to

HALLOWEEN FUN

and

TRICK-OR-TREATERS!

HALLOWEEN IS...

BY GAIL GIBBONS

Holiday House / New York

Printed and bound in October 2013 at Kwong Fat Offset Printing Co., Ltd.,
Dongguan City, Guang Dong Province, China.
www.holidayhouse.com
7 9 11 10 8
Library of Congress Cataloging-in-Publication Data
Gibbons, Gail.
Halloween is—/by Gail Gibbons.
p. cm.
Summary: Describes the origins and history
of Halloween traditions and festivities
from ancient times to the present day.
ISBN 0-8234-1758-1 (hardcover)
ISBN 0-8234-1797-2 (paperback)
1. Halloween—Juvenile literature.
[1. Halloween. 2. Holidays.] I. Title.
GT4965.G55 2002
394.2646—dc21 2001059429
ISBN-13: 978-0-8234-1758-2 (hardcover) ISBN-10: 0-8234-1758-1 (hardcover)
ISBN-13: 978-0-8234-1797-1 (paperback) ISBN-10: 0-8234-1797-2 (paperback)

HALLOWEEN IS...A FALL CELEBRATION.

Halloween started from many ancient beliefs and customs.
It is celebrated on October 31.

In ancient times, people feared the coming of winter. They were afraid the sun they worshiped would be killed by the darkness of the longer nights. It was a scary time of year.

They believed witches, goblins, ghosts, and other spirits roamed the earth, casting spells and playing evil tricks on people.

To avoid being recognized as humans when they left their homes after dark, some people wore costumes and masks to disguise themselves as fellow spirits. Others made big bonfires to scare away the evil spirits.

Years later, November 1 became a church holy day called
All Saints' Day, or All Hallows'. The evening before,
October 31, was called All Hallows' Eve. People continued
some of the old customs. Over time, All Hallows' Eve was
shortened to Halloween.

HALLOWEEN HAS MANY SYMBOLS.
HALLOWEEN IS...PUMPKINS.

Pumpkins come in all shapes and sizes. They are a symbol of autumn harvest.

ALWAYS have an adult help you when carving and lighting your pumpkin.

Many people like to carve pumpkins. They put candles or lights inside them. When they are lit, the pumpkins glow.

Some people call Halloween pumpkins jack-o'-lanterns. An old fable tells about a man named Jack who was selfish. When he died, he wasn't allowed into heaven.

The devil threw Jack a hot, glowing coal. Jack placed the shining coal inside a turnip he had carved. He roamed about the night, trying to find heaven. People called him Jack of the Lantern, or Jack-o'-lantern.

HALLOWEEN IS...HALLOWEEN DECORATIONS.

Halloween decorations are seen everywhere. Cornstalks, pumpkins, and gourds decorate homes and other places.

Many symbols of Halloween are put on doors, windows, and porches.

HALLOWEEN IS... MASKS AND COSTUMES, TOO.

It's time for make-believe! Some people dress up as witches.
Others dress up as ghosts or monsters.

All kinds of masks and costumes are seen on Halloween.
People can pretend to be anything they want to be.

HALLOWEEN IS...BATS,

Throughout history, people feared bats. Bats flew about in the night sky guided, it seemed, by a mysterious power. What people didn't understand, they feared.

BLACK CATS,

At one time, people believed that cats had magical powers and that witches' cats were black. They even thought witches could turn into cats.

AND SKELETONS!

Skeletons were scary. They reminded people of ghosts, evil spirits, and the dead. Today they are used to scare people and have fun.

HALLOWEEN IS...SCARY STORY TIME.

Weird and scary stories are enjoyed by all.

HALLOWEEN IS... "TRICK OR TREAT!"

In past times, some mischievous children would go from house to house dressed in costumes, asking for a "treat" and threatening a "trick" if they didn't get one. That's how the expression "Trick or treat!" began.

ALWAYS have an adult go trick-or-treating with you.

Today people have fun when Halloween trick-or-treaters come to their homes. They enjoy seeing the different costumes. Trick-or-treat bags are filled with Halloween treats.

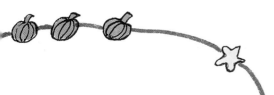

Often people celebrate Halloween by giving parties. It is fun to guess who is who.

AND HALLOWEEN GAMES.

Bobbing for apples is an old English game. There are many other games too.

HALLOWEEN IS... CANDIED APPLES

All kinds of party snacks are enjoyed. Yum!

HALLOWEEN IS...SCARY PLAYS

Some schools put on Halloween plays. Parents come to enjoy the fun.

AND HAUNTED HOUSES!

Sometimes there are make-believe haunted houses for guests
to go through. EEK!

HALLOWEEN IS...PARADES,

LAUGHTER, MAKE-BELIEVE, and time for saying...